T0195959

# THESE BEES!

## THE ADVENTURES OF SAM THE BACKYARD BEEKEEPER

WRITTEN BY NEELY CIARCIA

ILLUSTRATED BY BRIGHT JUNGLE STUDIOS

Copyright © 2020 Neely Ciarcia.

All rights reserved. No part of this book may be used or reproduced by any means, graphic, electronic, or mechanical, including photocopying, recording, taping or by any information storage retrieval system without the written permission of the author except in the case of brief quotations embodied in critical articles and reviews.

Archway Publishing books may be ordered through booksellers or by contacting:

Archway Publishing
1663 Liberty Drive
Bloomington, IN 47403
www.archwaypublishing.com
1 (888) 242-5904

Because of the dynamic nature of the Internet, any web addresses or links contained in this book may have changed since publication and may no longer be valid. The views expressed in this work are solely those of the author and do not necessarily reflect the views of the publisher, and the publisher hereby disclaims any responsibility for them.

Interior Image Credit: Bright Jungle Studios

ISBN: 978-1-4808-9378-8 (sc)
ISBN: 978-1-4808-9379-5 (e)

Print information available on the last page.

Archway Publishing rev. date: 08/20/2020

Sam had ALWAYS wanted to keep bees in his backyard. So one day he did! He thought bees were the coolest insects on earth.

Sam didn't know a lot about bees, but he knew they liked flowers, so he planted lots and lots of flowers all over his yard so the little bees could collect sweet nectar and **pollen** and make lots of honey.

Sam wasn't sure if bees liked a sunny or shady spot for their **hive**, so he found the perfect somewhat sunny, somewhat shady corner of his backyard.

One chilly Fall day, Sam was busy raking leaves when he heard a curious slight strumming, a louder hum-humm- humming and then a loud BUZZ--- BUZZ-BUZZING!!!!!

He dropped his rake and said "THESE BEES!" But because he loved his bees so much, he leaned in and listened very closely until he could hear the sound of thousands of tiny bee voices saying:

"We feel a breeze! We are cold! We need a sunnier spot and something to wrap our hive, pleeaasseee!!"

So Sam located a much sunnier place for the hive and wrapped the box in **burlap** to protect them from the cold winds coming with Winter.

As frosty Winter settled in and the days got colder, Sam decided the **Queen Bee** should come inside to a small box in the garage to stay warm—she IS the Queen after all! So he located her and gently removed her from the hive, settling her safe and cozy inside. He just knew she would be much happier now!

In the middle of a very dark snowy night later that week, Sam was suddenly awoken by an unmistakeable slight strumming, a louder hum-humm-humming and then a loud ʙᴜᴢᴢ--- BUZZ-BUZZING!!!!! Sam sat straight up in bed and said "THESE BEES!" But because he loved his bees so much, he leaned in and listened very closely until he could hear the sound of thousands of tiny bee voices saying:

"Where did you take our Queen? We NEED her! We don't know how to survive without her! We are **Queenless**!"

So Sam jumped out of his warm bed, pulled on his favorite sweatpants and rushed out to the garage where he was keeping the Queen nice and protected from the winter. He reluctantly returned her to the hive- now the hive was **Queenright** again! Sam knew to NEVER take the Queen from his bees again!

The Winter was long and cold, and the bees buzzed on, vibrating their wings to keep themselves and the hive warm and cozy. The beginning of Spring was a welcome change with it's bright and beautiful days. Sam went to check on his bees and saw they were happily and busily bustling around the hive. He gave them some sugar water to keep them fed until the flowers started to bloom. A few breezy and warm days later, Sam was cleaning out his garage and he heard the now familiar slight strumming, a louder hum-humm-humming and then a loud Buzz--- BUZZ—BUZZING!!!!!

He dropped his broom and said "THESE BEES!" But because he loved his bees so much, he leaned in and listened very closely until he could hear the sound of thousands of tiny bee voices saying:

"We are so crowded in here! We need more room! Please give us more space so we can spread out otherwise we will have to **swarm**!"

WELL! Sam still didn't know EVERYTHING about bees but he KNEW he did NOT want them to **swarm**- which means they would all leave the hive in a large group and never come back! So Sam quickly went down to the hive with a **super** and put the extra box on top so the bees could spread out.

As he was placing more **frames** into the super, Sam noticed one little bee got slightly pinched! He flew away quickly but probably had a little bee bruise. Suddenly something happened that had NEVER happened to Sam with his bees before. One of his bees STUNG him on the leg!

"OWWWWWW!" yelled Sam. He had been told once that bees are very sensitive to the energy around them so Sam had always been calm and peaceful and loving and gentle around his bees. When he was calm and peaceful and loving and gentle, the bees were too! Imagine that!

So what went wrong?!?

Suddenly as Sam was examining the bright red spot on his leg, he heard that slight strumming, a louder hum-humm-humming and then a loud Buzz—BUZZ---BUZZING!!!!!! Sam looked up and said "THESE BEES!"

But because he loved his bees so much, he leaned in and listened very closely until he could hear the sound of thousands of tiny bee voices saying:

"You hurt Bobby! Bobby is bruised! And when you hurt one of us, you hurt all of us! Please be more careful when you move things in our hive!"

Sam was AMAZED and had to go to his big BEE BOOK and read the chapter on this! He discovered that the bees have a **hive mind** and that they function as ONE bee even though there are thousands of them! Isn't that SO COOL? So when Bobby got hurt, all of the bees "felt" his pain.

Sam was sad he accidentally hurt one of his bees. He was very careful from then on every time he checked on the bees and moved anything around in their hive.

The Spring produced amazing flowers for the bees to flit about and the Summer came with heat and more fragrant flowers offering their nectar and pollen. The bees were in Bee Heaven! Sam thought "Phew! My bees are so happy now! I am the best backyard beekeeper in the world!" But one day, as Sam was setting up his grill for a BBQ with his favorite neighbors, he heard once again that slight strumming, a louder hum-humm-humming and then a loud Buzz--- BUZZ—BUZZING!!!!!

He firmly put down the grill brush and said "THESE BEES!" What could possibly be wrong now??? But because he loved his bees so much, he leaned in and listened very closely until he could hear the sound of thousands of tiny bee voices saying:

"We love you, too Sam!"

Bee Vocabulary Words:

**Burlap:** rough, brown woven fabric

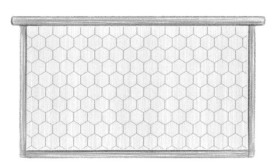

**Frames:** a rectangular piece of a hive that is where the bees store their honey and the Queen lays eggs

**Hive:** a place where bees are kept, usually a box or a dome

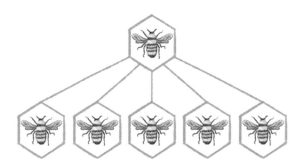

**Hive Mind:** the collective mental activity of a bee colony

**Pollen:** a yellow powdery substance found on the stamen of flowers

**Queen Bee:** the largest bee in the hive who is taken care of and fed and lays all the eggs

**Queenless:** a hive missing its Queen

**Queenright:** a hive with a Queen

**Super:** an extra box added to an existing hive

**Swarm:** when a Queen bee leaves a colony with a lot of worker bees

Printed in the United States
By Bookmasters